I'm Reading About

The WHITE HOUSE

GALLOPADE

by Carole Marsh

Printed and Manufactured in Peachtree City, GA., USA www.gallopade.com

Book design: Susan Van Denhende

Editor: Janice Baker

Photo Credits: Page 3: C.W. Fitzpatrick, U.S. Department of Defense. Page 7A: Zaplchigo/Bigstock.com; 7B: Albertdebruijn/Bigstock.com. Page 11A: Library of Congress; 11B: Asher B. Durand, U.S. Navy. Page 13: George Munger, White House Historical Association. Page 15A: George W. Bush White House Archives; 15B: The White House; 15C: Nixon Library. Page 17, Page 22A & E: Pete Souza, The Official White House Photostream. Page 18A: Empty Podium by Josh Berglund19, CC-BY 2.0; 18B: @realDonaldTrump on Twitter; 18C and Page 26: Pete Souza, White House Flickr Account. Page 20A: whitehouse.gov.; 20B: i.ytimg.com. Page 22B: William D. Moss, archive.defense.gov; 22C and Page 30D: Pete Souza, White House; 22D: White House Photo Office Collection (Nixon Administration), U.S. National Archives and Records Administration. Page 24: CityPhotosbyRod/Bigstock.com. Pages 28 and 30F: Cecil Stoughton, U.S. National Archives and Records Administration. Page 30A: Library of Congress; 30B: Barbara Kinney, Clinton Presidential Library and Museum; 30C: topics.blogs.nytimes.com; 30E: presidentialpetmuseum.com. Page 32A: Chuck Kennedy, White House Flickr Account; 32B: White House Photographic Office, U.S. National Archives and Records Administration; 32C: whitehouse.gov. Page 34: Carol M. Highsmith, Library of Congress

The White House is where the President of the United States lives and works.

What is so special about the White House?

Let's read about it and see!

LOCATION

The White House is located
in Washington, D.C.

Washington, D.C., is the capital of the United States.
It is the home of America's government.
America's laws are made there!

Washington, D.C., is named after George Washington.
He was the first President of the United States.

Washington, D.C.
Here it is!

ENTRANCES

The White House has two main entrances.

The north entrance is like the front door to a house. The President meets important guests there.

The south entrance is like the back door to a house. It looks out over the South Lawn, which is the "backyard." Lots of fun activities take place on the South Lawn!

Each entrance is covered by a porch known as a "portico."

White House

DIAGRAM

The White House has buildings attached to both sides of it:

- Executive Residence – where the President lives
- East and West Colonnades – hallways
- The West Wing – offices for the President and staff
- The East Wing – offices for the First Lady and others

An underground bunker lies under the East Wing. The President can go there in an emergency!

White House Complex

HISTORY

Workers began building the White House in 1792.
It took eight years to finish it.

President George Washington chose the location.
He approved the design too.
But he never lived there!

In 1800, President John Adams moved in
with his wife Abigail.
He was the first President to live
in the White House!

First Resident

President John Adams

HISTORY

During the War of 1812,
something terrible happened to the White House.
British soldiers set it on fire!
Luckily, the White House did not burn down completely.
A strong thunderstorm put out the fire!

After the fire, only the outside walls
and inside brick walls remained.
It took three years to rebuild the White House.

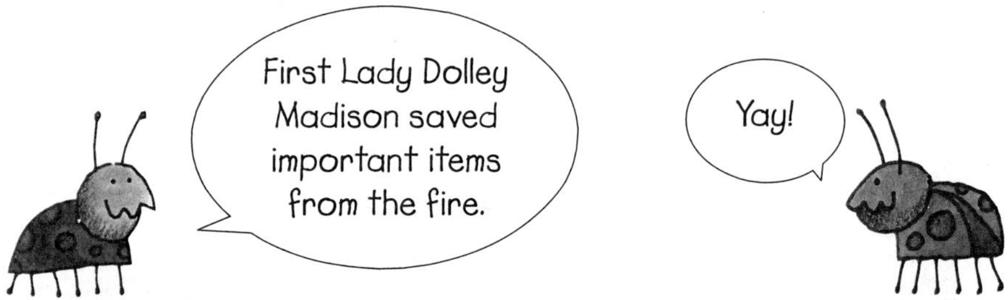

Fire in 1814

BY THE NUMBERS

What is inside the White House?

- 6 floors
- 132 rooms and 35 bathrooms
- 412 doors, 147 windows, and 28 fireplaces
- 8 staircases and 3 elevators

The 6 floors include
2 floors for the First Family,
2 public floors, and 2 basements.

Big House

I am the Oval Office.
I am the President's office!
You will find me in the West Wing
of the White House Complex.

I usually get a new look
when a new President is elected.
They like to redecorate me!
Do you like my rounded walls?

Oval Office

Places for Business

Press Briefing Room

Cabinet Room

Situation Room

Important business takes place in the White House! There are special rooms for special business.

Here are a few examples:

- Situation Room – for decisions in crisis situations
- Cabinet Room – for meetings of the President's advisors
- Press Briefing Room – for press conferences

The Situation Room is nicknamed the "Sit Room."

Rose Garden

GARDEN

I am the Rose Garden!
I am full of gorgeous roses and many other flowers.
You can find me just outside the Oval Office.
Presidents use me for special ceremonies and speeches.

One of my favorite events was when
President Nixon's daughter Tricia was married here!

Having Fun

RECREATION

How do you like to relax?
Watch a movie? Play some ball?

The President can do that too.
Right in the White House!
Yes, it's true!

The White House has lots of fun spots
for the President, his family, and guests:

Putting Green

Jogging Track

Movie Theater

Bowling Alley

Basketball Court

And More!

Landing Pad

HELICOPTER

I am Marine One!
I am the President's helicopter.

I provide a very handy way to travel.
The South Lawn is my helipad.
That is where I take off and land.

The President can walk out of the Oval Office
and hop on board!

Marine One's glass and body
are resistant to bullets!

South Lawn

SOUTH LAWN

I am the South Lawn.
I am the place for lots of fun!
I host many lively events.

The annual Easter Egg Roll is
the most famous event held here.
Kids and adults gather for a big Easter party!

Other fun events on my lawn include:

Concerts **Barbeques** **Campouts** **Tee Ball** **And More!**

Family Life

FAMILIES

The President's family is known as
the "First Family."
Many First Families have lived in the White House!

- Some Presidents had big families, like Theodore Roosevelt.
- Some Presidents had young families, like John F. Kennedy.
- Some Presidents even had grandchildren, like John Adams!

One thing is for sure—
all the First Kids liked to play and have fun.
Just like you!

Presidential Pets

Presidents and their kids love pets!
Pets of all kinds have lived in the White House:

Dogs **Cats** **Hamsters** **Parakeets** **Rabbits** **And More!**

President Theodore Roosevelt and his 6 kids had the most pets—about 30!

Holidays

The White House has special holiday traditions—
just like you do!

Each Thanksgiving, the President pardons a turkey.
That lucky turkey goes to live on a farm—
never to be eaten for Thanksgiving!

Every Christmas, glittering decorations
fill the house from top to bottom.
Some Presidents have had more than
25 Christmas trees!

Visiting the White House

VISITORS

Did you know the White House is called
the "People's House"?
It belongs to all Americans!

You can visit the White House.
Tours are available five days per week.
You have to make a special request in advance.
There are no surprise visits to the White House!

GLOSSARY

bunker: an underground shelter with strong walls to protect the people inside it

Cabinet: a group of people who give advice to a country's leader

colonnade: a row of tall columns that support a building or roof

crisis: a time of difficulty when important decisions need to be made

helipad: a special place where a helicopter can take off and land

pardon: to release from punishment

press conference: a meeting where someone gives information to news reporters

redecorate: to change the appearance of the inside of a room or house